HEY DIDDLE DIDDLE

Sam Foster

summersdale

HEY DIDDLE DIDDLE

Illustrations by Lora Redman

With thanks to Ianthe Butt and Gemma Halder

Summersdale Publishers Ltd
46 West Street
Chichester
West Sussex
PO19 1RP
UK

www.summersdale.com

Printed and bound in the UK by
CPI Mackays, Chatham ME5 8TD

ISBN: 978-1-84024-708-4

HEY DIDDLE DIDDLE

OUR BEST-LOVED NURSERY RHYMES
AND
WHAT THEY REALLY MEAN

Sam Foster

CONTENTS

INTRODUCTION

Whether you grew up singing and dancing to them, or having them recited to you as you were tucked up in bed, everybody remembers their favourite nursery rhymes.

Passed down through the generations from parents to children, nursery rhymes charm and entertain us. With their colourful characters and seemingly simple lyrics, they spark our young imaginations and, as we get older, evoke happy childhood memories as we create new ones with our own offspring.

Many nursery rhymes were merely tongue twisters or innovative games, devised to widen vocabulary or improve pronunciation skills. Others, however, have dramatic, hidden meanings nestling between their childish images and seemingly nonsensical words, with

7

most originating as veiled commentaries on political events and social evils.

The ditties of our early days take on new meanings through subtle references and clever wordplay and, like a big screen blockbuster, nursery rhymes have it all: excitement, royal scandal, illicit love affairs, bloodshed and comedy. Versions vary widely, but this book includes the most commonly known.

Dust down your memories on this whirlwind tour through history, stopping off at a few rather unexpected and unusual destinations, as you discover the fascinating true stories and the speculated meanings behind these classic nursery rhymes.

HEY DIDDLE DIDDLE

Hey diddle diddle,
The cat and the fiddle,
The cow jumped over the
moon;
The little dog laughed
To see such fun,
And the dish ran away with the
spoon.

This seemingly ridiculous rhyme, first published in 1765, is said to describe Elizabethan court life, with the cat being Queen Elizabeth I, who manipulated or 'fiddled' her cabinet members like a cat with a mouse between its paws.

The little dog would be Robert Dudley, the Earl of Leicester, whom Elizabeth called her 'lap dog' and for whom she had a particular soft spot.

It is speculated that the dish running away with the spoon refers to the scandalous elopement of Elizabeth's serving lady with the royal 'taster'. After catching the illicit lovers, Elizabeth imprisoned the pair in the Tower of London as punishment for inappropriate behaviour. But what of the cow and the moon?

Another theory is that the rhyme is astrological – as well as the Moon, nearly all of the characters correspond to star constellations:

The cat – Leo the Lion

The fiddle – Lyra the Lyre

The cow – Taurus the Bull

The little dog – Canis Minor, the Lesser Dog

The dish – The Crater

The spoon – Ursa Major, the Big Dipper

Interestingly, these constellations are only visible simultaneously in the night sky during April, and it is said that English farmers, on seeing this combination, knew it was time to begin sowing their crops.

> Nicknames were common to mask the identities of court members, who were subject to much gossip and intrigue.

Alternatively, the meaning could be found in the animal-headed gods and goddesses of ancient Egyptian mythology: the cat-goddess Bast, often pictured with her sistrum (a stringed instrument similar to a fiddle); the cow-deity Hathor, often depicted with the sun's orb between his horns (which the author could have misinterpreted as a moon); the little dog would be jackal-headed Anubis, while the dish and the spoon were important in many ancient Egyptian religious rites.

But, more prosaically, maybe 'Hey Diddle Diddle' refers to a pub crawl route originating in the eighteenth century which took place along the Macclesfield–Buxton road. Now the A537, the route is a favourite among bikers, and still home to some of the pubs mentioned, all built in the 1700s by a group of rich quarry owners.

The Half Moon stopped trading long ago, but The Cat and the Fiddle public house is still in business, and the third, The Setter Dog, closed in 2002. Anyone who had visited all three would have consumed a few tankards of ale and would indeed have been having lots of fun. The final pub on the route is The Dish and Spoon, which currently trades under the name The Peak View Tearooms.

HARK, HARK, THE DOGS DO BARK

Hark, hark,
The dogs do bark,
The beggars are coming to town;
Some in rags,
And some in jags,
And one in a velvet gown.

In thirteenth-century England, a large proportion of the population was unemployed and droves of beggars descended on the towns, setting dogs barking. Vagrants came dressed in whatever they could get their hands on – everything from rags through to expensive coats.

'Hark, hark' tells the townspeople to listen well to the beggars, as they often sang songs and told stories which contained secret messages. Songs were frequently used as a vehicle to covertly pass propaganda between towns, sometimes leading to uprisings and rebellions against those in power.

Some say, however, that the rhyme may allude to Henry VIII dissolving the monasteries when England made the shift from Catholicism to the Church of England. When Henry's men raided the monasteries, seizing their land and pocketing their riches, the monks suddenly found themselves destitute. Thrust out of their home, and with no income, the monks became wandering beggars. Their odd 'rags' and 'jags' attire would depend on whatever they could find, as they would no longer be able to wear monastic dress.

'Jags' were slits made in clothing to reveal a flash of a different colour underneath. Whether the beggars intended to have jags, or their clothes were just ripped, is another matter.

LITTLE MISS MUFFET

Little Miss Muffet
Sat on a tuffet,
Eating her curds and whey;
There came a big spider,
Who sat down beside her
And frightened Miss Muffet away.

Dr Thomas Muffet (1553–1604) was a renowned entomologist and author of the first catalogue of native British insects, *The Theatre of Insects*. He was fascinated by spiders, keeping them around the house as pets. The young Miss Patience Muffet, not sharing her stepfather's love of creepy crawlies, was evidently startled when one of them crawled up beside her during breakfast – perhaps the first documented instance of someone with arachnophobia.

When milk is curdled with something acidic, such as vinegar or lemon juice, it produces a liquid known as whey, and the solid lumps within it are the curds – nowadays it goes by the name of cottage cheese.

However, others say that Little Miss Muffet may symbolise Mary, Queen of Scots (1542–1587) and the spider a minister named John Knox, who was a devout and vocal Protestant during the years leading up to the Scottish Reformation, and never trusted the Roman Catholic queen. Due to their religious differences, Knox was keen to frighten Mary from her throne – likened here to a 'tuffet'.

A 'tuffet', originally a small hillock or mound of grass-covered earth, had come to mean a low seat covered completely in cushioned fabric (also known as a pouffe or hassock).

DING, DONG, BELL

Ding, dong, bell,
Pussy's in the well.
Who put her in?
Little Johnny Flynn.
Who pulled her out?
Little Tommy Stout.

What a naughty boy was that,
To try to drown poor pussy cat,
Who never did any harm,
And killed the mice in his
       farmer's barn.

There is some dispute over Johnny's surname: he is also sometimes known as Johnny Thin (presumably in contrast to the fatter Tommy Stout), or Johnny Green.

This rhyme dates back to the sixteenth century, and the phrase 'Ding, dong, bell' was used in several Shakespeare plays, for example *The Tempest*:

'Sea nymphs hourly ring his knell:

Hark! Now I hear them – Ding, dong, bell.'

It's possible the song refers to the medieval practice of the ducking stool, which continued even into the early nineteenth century. Ducking under water was a punishment used on women perceived to be morally dubious, such as gossips or prostitutes. 'Pussy' was a term used to describe a loose woman, as cats were associated with lust, chaos and the female form. The woman would be paraded through the streets to a cacophony of banging pots and pans, and pealing church bells, to attract the attention of the community. The procession went to the village well-pond, and 'pussy' was repeatedly lowered into the water by the young men of the village.

The last couplet has a slightly different rhythm, so it may have been added later in the eighteenth century when many old nursery rhymes were collected, modified and written down. The original lyrics ended with the cat being left to drown, whereas the later version provides a moral lesson to children to discourage cruelty to animals who 'never did any harm'.

REMEMBER, REMEMBER

Remember, remember the fifth of November,
Gunpowder, treason and plot.
I see no reason why gunpowder, treason
Should ever be forgot...

On 5 November 1605, Guy Fawkes, along with nine fellow conspirators, was caught red-handed in an attempt to blow up King James I during the State Opening of the Houses of Parliament, after stashing dozens of barrels of gunpowder in the cellar. The men were Catholics, whose religion had been persecuted by the Protestant monarch.

Fawkes was found guilty of high treason – a crime which carried the horrific punishment of being hung, drawn and quartered. Prisoners were hanged by the neck but taken down while still alive, then had their genitals and bowels cut out and burned in front of them. Finally, the beheading would take place, and the remaining body would be quartered – chopped into four parts.

Although weakened by torture, Guy managed to avoid all this by jumping from the gallows when the noose was tied around his neck, which was broken, and he died instantly.

The date of 5 November is also an important symbol in the futuristic graphic novel *V for Vendetta*, written by Alan Moore and illustrated by David Lloyd. A mysterious figure dressed as Guy Fawkes tries to bring down a totalitarian government in Britain. *V for Vendetta* was made into a film in 2006, starring Natalie Portman and Hugo Weaving.

To this day, across England on the fifth of November, the thwarting of the Gunpowder Plot is commemorated with fireworks and bonfires, on which a stuffed 'guy' is burnt. Children stuff old clothes with newspaper or straw to make the figure of a man. Originally, it was not Guy Fawkes that was burnt on the fires but an effigy of the Pope. This practice still continues in the town of Lewes, East Sussex, with other unpopular figures burnt alongside the Pope Paul V effigy (most notoriously, an Osama Bin Laden guy was burnt in 2001). However, in York – Guy Fawkes' hometown – they do not burn a guy on the official city bonfire.

JACK BE NIMBLE

Jack be nimble,
Jack be quick,
Jack jump over
The candlestick.

This rhyme might also have a connection to Black Jack – an English pirate in the sixteenth century who was famed for evading capture by the authorities, hence 'Jack be nimble'.

Candle-leaping was once a sport and a form of fortune-telling in England. Lace-makers in Wendover, Buckinghamshire, performed a strange ritual of jumping over candlesticks for good luck on St Catherine's Day (25 November). If the flame did not go out, it was thought that they would enjoy good fortune in the following year. If the flame was extinguished, they would be cursed with bad luck. This practice originated from the older, more dangerous version of jumping over fires.

Some believe the rhyme may refer to yellow fever, otherwise known as yellow jack fever, though this was spread by mosquitoes, so only usually occurred in warmer European climes. It was thought that the virus could be warded off by flames, so candles would be placed by children's bedsides.

A WISE OLD OWL

A wise old owl lived in an oak;
The more he saw the less he spoke;
The less he spoke the more he heard.
Why can't we all be like that wise old bird?

This nursery rhyme has a very clear message for children – that they should be quiet, like the owl. The proverb 'children should be seen and not heard' came into common use in English around the fifteenth century and, during Victorian times, children were expected to learn to hold their tongues and abstain from rowdy behaviour.

The owl has been considered a wise figure since the time of the Ancient Greeks, when Athena, the goddess of wisdom as well as war, was frequently depicted carrying the bird. The owl was also often regarded as a symbol of Athens, appearing on coins. The connection still remains and is reflected in the Latin names of a number of owls: the Burrowing Owl is the *Athene cunicularia*, and the Little Owl is *Athene noctua*.

Owls are the unofficial mascot of Mensa, the high IQ society.

The impression of the owl as thoughtful also comes from the patient manner in which it hunts its prey, remaining motionless and quiet until the perfect opportunity for a kill arises.

In World War Two the United States Army adopted this idea of the owl as a silent hunter, producing a poster using the rhyme, but changed the last line to 'Soldier… be like that old bird!' with the caption: 'Silence means security'.

HOT CROSS BUNS

Hot cross buns!
Hot cross buns!
One ha'penny, two ha'penny,
Hot cross buns!
If you have no daughters
Give them to your sons;
One ha'penny, two ha'penny,
Hot cross buns!

> The half penny coin was used in Britain for 700 years and was taken out of circulation in 1969.

Street sellers of the nineteenth century hawked their wares by shouting out the name of their produce. Hot cross buns, sweet spiced cakes made with currants and raisins with a white cross marked on top in flour or icing, were traditionally eaten on Good Friday in remembrance of the crucifixion. The song was sung by children as they ate the buns for breakfast at Easter.

The first recorded use of the term 'hot cross buns' was in 1733, although the buns may have their origins in pre-Christian traditions and could date back as far as the Saxon period, when buns would have been made in honour of the goddess Eostre, and the cross may have symbolised the four quarters of the moon. The Czech Republic also has an Easter cake marked with a cross.

For an innocent-looking cake, hot cross buns have proved surprisingly controversial over the years. Protestant monarch Elizabeth I viewed them as a threatening hangover of Catholicism – she thought the spicing was reminiscent of incense and the cross an example of Catholic symbolism. The queen seemed to take a killjoy exception to all buns, declaring it forbidden to 'make, utter, or sell' any 'spice cakes, buns, biscuits, or other spice bread'. Hot cross buns, however, proved too popular to be banned completely, so Elizabeth allowed bakeries to sell them at Easter and Christmas only.

Similarly, in 2003, several local councils in Britain banned hot cross buns on the grounds that the symbol could prove offensive to non-Christians.

LUCY LOCKET

Lucy Locket lost her pocket,
Kitty Fisher found it;
Not a penny was there in it,
Only ribbon round it.

Lucy Locket is believed to have worked as a barmaid in the Cock public house in London's Fleet Street. The Cock was established in 1554 and rebuilt in 1888 and was mentioned in the diary of Samuel Pepys. A 'pocket' was an old Middle English word for a small pouch for keeping money in. 'Ladies of the night' concealed their earnings in a pocket worn on the thigh, kept in place by a ribbon garter.

Kitty Fisher – or Catherine Maria 'Kitty' Fisher to give her full name – was a famous courtesan who died in 1767. She was a model and aspiring actress, known for her good looks, wit and equestrian skills. On a visit to England, the notorious Italian adventurer Casanova was impressed by her beauty and finery, remarking, 'She was magnificently dressed… She had on diamonds worth five hundred thousand francs.'

Nathaniel Hone's painting of Kitty Fisher hangs in the National Portrait Gallery in London and shows her alongside a kitten trying to paw a fish in a bowl.

In this rhyme, it seems one of Lucy's lovers no longer has the money to afford her services, so she 'lost her pocket' to Kitty, who might have found the 'ribbon' around him – his clothes and good looks – were enough to keep her interested.

This seems questionable, as diamond-loving Kitty is rumoured to have charged a strict £100 fee per customer. The Duke of Cumberland offered her a mere £50 for her services, and an affronted Kitty showed her disdain by buttering two slices of bread and eating the Duke's £50 note between them.

The tune for 'Lucy Locket' was later used for the American song 'Yankee Doodle', which is the state anthem of Connecticut.

RING-A-RING O' ROSES

Ring-a-ring o' roses,
A pocket full of posies,
A-tishoo! A-tishoo!
We all fall down.

Commonly sung in school playgrounds, 'Ring-a-Ring o' Roses' is widely believed to describe the unpleasant red ring-shaped rash symptomatic of the bubonic plague.

The Great Plague of London in 1665 was spread by rats carrying infected fleas, and a common, but incorrect, belief at the time was that it was transmitted by bad odours, so people stuffed their pockets fit to burst with pungent herbs and 'posies'. Smoking copious amounts of tobacco and pepper and heady frankincense were also encouraged in the hope that they might cleanse the air.

'A-tishoo! A-tishoo!' mimics the violent sneezing which was another symptom of the disease. 'We all fall down' highlights the indiscriminate nature of the Plague – anyone, irrespective of age or wealth, was liable to be struck down. The 1665 epidemic is estimated to have wiped out a staggering 75,000–100,000 people, a fifth of the population of London.

> Ironically, but on a happier note, despite the rather sinister origins of this rhyme, countless wedding boutiques and flower shops choose to name themselves Ring-a-Ring o' Roses.

Folklorists say the rhyme was sung by adolescents during the eighteenth century, who craftily invented circle games – joining hands and skipping in a circle – in order to avoid the dancing bans imposed by strict Protestants.

HUMPTY DUMPTY

Humpty Dumpty sat on a wall,
Humpty Dumpty had a great fall.
All the king's horses,
And all the king's men,
Couldn't put Humpty together again.

The phrase 'Humpty Dumpty' would have been familiar in the Middle Ages, long before the rhyme, as a slang expression for a clumsy, obese or hunchbacked person.

The most popular interpretation of the nursery rhyme, however, is that Humpty Dumpty was the nickname of a Royalist cannon used during the English Civil War (1642–1649). The cannon sat on the wall of a church in Colchester, until being blown to smithereens by the attacking Parliamentarians. Despite the best efforts of the Royalist infantry and cavalry – 'All the king's horses, And all the king's men' – the cannon was left in pieces.

In the 1700s, a heady concoction of beer, port and brandy was known as a 'Humptie Dumptie', which undoubtedly induced a drunken clumsiness that might cause you to topple…

The current perception of Humpty Dumpty as an egg came about after Lewis Carroll famously portrayed a figure as such in his 1871 storybook *Through the Looking-glass*.

Later, in 1902, the rhyme appeared as a riddle in *Mother Goose Nursery Rhymes*, with a fifth line, 'what was Humpty?', being added. The correct answer was 'an egg', with 'all the king's horses and all the king's men' referring to the toast soldiers used for dipping into the yolk. Riddling rhymes had been popular for many centuries and would have almost certainly been in existence orally long before publication.

The Penguin character from the *Batman* comics, played by Danny DeVito in the popular nineties films, is said to have been inspired by Humpty Dumpty. His similarities to a Humpty figure are reflected in his hunchback, awkward manner and obsession for taking things apart and putting them back together again.

BAA, BAA, BLACK SHEEP

Baa, baa, black sheep,
Have you any wool?
Yes, sir, yes, sir,
Three bags full;
One for my master,
And one for my dame,
And one for the little boy
Who lives down the lane.

First published in 1744, this well-loved verse has its historical origins in ancient tax laws.

In 1275, King Edward began to collect a duty known as 'The Great Custom' on all exports of wool. One third would be given to 'the master', meaning the king; one third to 'the dame', being the Church or local nobility, and the final third for 'the little boy' would be the meagre amount that workers could keep for themselves.

'Baa, Baa, Black Sheep' lent its name to a television show created by Stephen J. Cannell which aired between 1976 and 1978, about the World War Two experiences of aviator 'Pappy' Boyington and his Marine Corps troop, known as the 'Black Sheep Squadron'.

The BBC believes that a crackly version of 'Baa, Baa, Black Sheep', recorded in 1951, is the oldest piece of computer-generated music. The recording was made by a Ferranti Mark 1, the world's third commercially available computer, which at the time of production cost more to buy than an entire fleet of luxury cars.

In 2000, Birmingham City Council tried to ban 'Baa, Baa, Black Sheep', claiming it contained negative stereotypes about the black community. Local black families, however, dismissed the claims as ridiculous and the council withdrew the ban. The rhyme hit the headlines again in 2006, when several nurseries in Britain, also believing it to have racist connotations, changed the first line to 'Baa, Baa, rainbow sheep' or 'Baa, Baa, happy sheep'.

GRAND OLD DUKE OF YORK

Oh, the grand old Duke of York,
He had ten thousand men;
He marched them up to the top of the hill,
And he marched them down again.

And when they were up, they were up,
And when they were down, they were down,
And when they were only half-way up,
They were neither up nor down.

The Duke of York was Richard Plantagenet, and the song mocks his defeat at the Battle of Wakefield during the War of the Roses.

Richard marched his army to Sandal Castle, on the site of an old Norman motte-and-bailey fortress. A motte was an artificial hill constructed from earth, and Sandal's motte stood 33 feet above normal ground level. The soil would have come from a deep ditch, dug to surround the castle as an extra obstacle for approaching enemies.

> Richard Plantagenet is believed to be the same Richard aptly immortalised in the mnemonic we use to remember the colours of the rainbow: Richard Of York Gave Battle In Vain (Red Orange Yellow Green Blue Indigo Violet).

Richard, with his army of only 5,000–8,000 men (exaggerated to 10,000 in the rhyme), decided to 'march them down again' from the safety of the castle to the bottom of the hill – straight into direct combat with the Lancastrian forces who outnumbered Richard's troops threefold, and completely overwhelmed them. The Duke's illogical decision to leave higher ground cost him not only the battle, but also his own life and those of more than one third of his troops.

Scouts and other groups of children sing the song to the melody of 'A-Hunting We Will Go', complete with the actions of standing up, sitting down and marching when appropriate.

LITTLE BO-PEEP

Little Bo-peep has lost her sheep,
And doesn't know where to find them;
Leave them alone, and they'll come home,
Bringing their tails behind them.

Little Bo-peep fell fast asleep,
And dreamt she heard them bleating;
But when she awoke, she found it a joke,
For they were all still fleeting.

Then up she took her little crook,
Determined for to find them;
She found them indeed, but it made her
                        heart bleed,
For they left their tails behind them.

It happened one day, as Bo-peep did stray
Into a meadow hard by,
There she espied their tails side by side,
All hung on a tree to dry.

She heaved a sigh, and wiped her eye,
And over the hillocks went rambling,
And tried what she could, as a shepherdess
                                        should,
To tack again each to its lambkin.

During the eighteenth century, smuggling was rife in the English town of St Leonards, near Hastings. Captured culprits were detained in the Martello Tower, nicknamed 'Bo-peep', the official residence of the queen's customs officials. The lost sheep were the smugglers, and the 'tails' were most likely barrels of brandy, or rum, which would often be left behind if the smugglers believed that they were under suspicion.

Customs officials were always keen to catch criminals, even when they'd abandoned their loot, and the tacking of the 'tails' back onto the sheep were their attempts to match contraband to smugglers and apprehend them successfully.

Interestingly, 'Little Bo-peep' is still used as Cockney rhyming slang for sheep.

Bo-peep also made an appearance as cowboy Woody's love interest in the popular 1990s Disney *Toy Story* movies as a sweet-natured porcelain doll, complete with her own flock of ceramic sheep.

POLLY PUT THE KETTLE ON

Polly put the kettle on,
Polly put the kettle on,
Polly put the kettle on,
We'll all have tea.

Sukey take it off again,
Sukey take it off again,
Sukey take it off again,
They've all gone away.

It seems this simple song was written in the eighteenth century by a father about the arguments between his five children. The boisterous boys wanted to play war games, and the girls didn't really want them around.

When Polly and Sukey (an eighteenth-century middle-class equivalent to the names Susan or Lily) wanted to get rid of their rowdy brothers, they would pretend to host a tea party. Promptly, the boys would leave, so as not to be roped into playing girly games, and peace and quiet was restored.

Their father was so entertained by the girls' cunning ploy to be rid of their brothers that he put it into words and composed a tune to go with it.

> In Charles Dickens' novel *Barnaby Rudge*, the character of Grip the raven quotes this poem. Grip was a real pet raven of the Dickens family who loved to talk – with 'Polly put the kettle on' being one of his favourite expressions.

It became a well-known country dance tune, and the Irish/English reel based on the song, printed in *Variations for the Pianoforte* was, according to collector John Glen, 'very popular with young ladies'. On the polar expedition led by Admiral Parry in 1810, a barrel organ was brought on ship to provide entertainment and exercise through dancing, and this was one of eight tunes on it.

GOOSEY, GOOSEY GANDER

Goosey, goosey gander,
Whither shall I wander?
Upstairs and downstairs
And in my Lady's chamber.
There I met an old man
Who would not say his prayers.
So I took him by his left leg
And threw him down the stairs.

For a funny nursery rhyme, 'Goosey, Goosey Gander' has macabre roots. 'Goosey' is a reference to the military marching goose-step of Oliver Cromwell's Roundhead army, which persecuted Catholics during the sixteenth century. On their marches, they would search houses 'upstairs and downstairs' in the hope of arresting or killing anyone who refused to convert to Puritanism.

The 'Lady's chamber' was a concealed closet, sometimes found in the bedrooms of wealthy women, and was otherwise known as a 'priest hole', as Catholic priests sought refuge in them. The complicit family were liable to be executed for such deception, if discovered.

> The rhyme could also be read to have sexual connotations, with 'goose' during the Tudor period being slang for a prostitute. 'Goose bumps' was a reference to the unpleasant warts associated with venereal disease. This could have been a warning about getting caught in the sack with someone unsavoury!

The refusal of this priest to 'say his prayers' was a common situation, as he would have been asked to recite his prayers in English (as was the Protestant tradition) as opposed to Latin (the Catholic way) to indicate his conversion.

'Left leg' was a derogatory nickname for Catholics, but was also a term for the brutal punishment to which they were subjected. A common punishment was to tie a rope round the leg of the accused, then to throw them down the stairs, hauling them up and down repeatedly. Torture would continue until a confession or death occurred – whichever came first.

According to Katherine Elwes Thomas, in her 1930 book *The Many Personages of Mother Goose*, this rhyme may refer specifically to one Cardinal Beaton, who refused conversion and was pushed down a flight of stairs and then viciously stabbed to death. Just to further their point, the Roundheads hung his lifeless body from the walls of a nearby castle. The message of this rhyme was a clear warning to all Catholics.

CHRISTMAS IS COMING

Christmas is coming, the geese are getting fat,
Please put a penny in the old man's hat;
If you haven't got a penny, a ha'penny will do,
If you haven't got a ha'penny then God bless
you!

During Victorian times, goose would have been the main dish on the Christmas menu of the masses. Turkey, introduced to Britain from America by landowner William Strickland in 1526, was expensive and only affordable for the rich upper classes. It wasn't until the early twentieth century that turkeys became affordable enough to grace the majority of British Christmas spreads.

In *A Christmas Carol*, Charles Dickens describes how the Cratchit family saved with the 'Goose Club', putting money aside throughout the year in order to be able to afford a bird at Christmas time. When Scrooge finally shuns his miserly ways, his wealth is indicated when he orders an expensive turkey for the family to eat.

This festive nursery rhyme sends the message that Christmas, as well as being a celebration, should be a time to 'put a penny in the old man's hat' and remember the less fortunate in the community. People are encouraged to be kind and give as much or as little as they can afford to, and if they don't have any money – which many people in the Victorian times wouldn't have had – then a simple 'God bless you' would suffice.

RIDE A COCK-HORSE TO BANBURY CROSS

Ride a cock-horse to Banbury Cross,
To see a fine lady upon a white horse;
With rings on her fingers and bells on her toes,
And she shall have music wherever she goes.

This rhyme is something of a mystery, although there are plenty of theories!

Was this fine lady Queen Elizabeth I, adorned with finery? The custom of attaching a small bell to each shoe first came into practice during the Plantagenet era and continued for some time within British nobility. Local minstrels would have provided the music by accompanying her, singing her praises. The cross in question is said to have been ripped down in the sixteenth century, although others have since been built on the same site.

The story goes that the queen was on her way to visit the large cross erected on a hilltop in the town of Banbury when her carriage wheel broke and she was left stranded. Spirited Elizabeth chose to mount the horse which had been pulling the carriage and ride instead.

> The 'cock-horse' was a hardworking horse attached to carriages at the bottom of hills to aid in steep ascents, and unhitched again at the top; in Banbury, the town council made a cock-horse available to help people to access the town.

Or was this fine lady the Lady Godiva? Her husband, the Earl of Mercia, enforced severely high taxes upon his subjects, which she thought unfair. She pleaded with her husband to either do away with the taxes or at least reduce them. Eventually, he struck a bargain with her: he would reassess his taxation laws if she would ride through Coventry stark naked on horseback – though the reason for this is unclear. Gutsy Godiva did just that, and rode through the town wearing only 'rings on her fingers and bells on her toes'. Some versions of the rhyme give Coventry, rather than Banbury, as the location, making Godiva a possible contender.

Horse goddess Rhiannon, featured in the Mabinogion, a collection of prose stories from medieval Welsh manuscripts, is also associated by some with the origins of this rhyme. She married a Welsh king, but when she bore a child, he was stolen from her. Falsely, she was blamed for his disappearance and was even accused of eating her own flesh and blood; as punishment she had to tell visitors about her crime and carry them on her back round the town. Rhiannon was described as riding a beautiful white horse which no one could catch, possibly the cock-horse described in the rhyme.

RAIN, RAIN, GO AWAY

Rain, rain, go away,
Come again another day.

Rain, rain, go to Spain,
Never show your face again.

During the Elizabethan era, the fierce rivalry between Spain and England came to a head with the Spanish launching a fleet of armed ships in an attempt to invade England in 1588. That the Spanish Armada was defeated was due partly to the speed of the smaller English vessels, and partly to heavy rainstorms which scattered the Spanish fleet and left them more vulnerable to English attacks. Any ships that survived would have headed back home to Spain, hence the line 'Rain, rain, go to Spain'.

A song based on the nursery rhyme, with music by Noel Regney and lyrics by Gloria Shayne Baker, was first recorded by Bobby Vinton. Since then, several rock bands, including Nine Inch Nails, Counting Crows and Breaking Benjamin, have used lines from the rhyme in chart-topping songs.

SING A SONG OF SIXPENCE

Sing a song of sixpence,
A pocket full of rye;
Four and twenty blackbirds,
Baked in a pie.
When the pie was opened,
The birds began to sing;
Was not that a dainty dish,
To set before the king?

The king was in his counting-house,
Counting out his money;
The queen was in the parlour,
Eating bread and honey.
The maid was in the garden,
Hanging out the clothes,
When down came a blackbird,
And pecked off her nose.

This rhyme pays homage to a custom of the fifteenth and sixteenth centuries. In the households of the gentry, it was regarded as a hilarious practical joke to bake live birds in a pie, so that they might fly out as the pie was cut open. The wedding of Henry IV of France and Marie de Medici in 1600 contained a similar spectacle – with songbirds flying out of the guests' folded napkins.

Like most nursery rhymes, this would have been popular amongst the common people, and it indicates some feelings of resentment towards royalty. The king and queen in the song have a languid existence, spending their time counting money and eating bread and honey. But why the poor maid should have been on the receiving end of the blackbird's revenge is a mystery.

When they weren't being used for party entertainment, blackbirds and other songbirds would also have been eaten as a delicacy.

It was claimed by website www.snopes.com that the rhyme was a coded message to recruit buccaneers for Blackbeard's pirate ships, and would have been sung in the taverns of various ports. The writers said the 'rye' referred not to the grain itself (which might have been used to feed blackbirds) but to whisky, distilled from rye – an added temptation for men to join the voyage. The blackbirds, they said, were Blackbeard's crew; and flying out of the pie suggested the speed and element of surprise with which they would have accosted their victims. Later, the website's creators said it was all a hoax created to test their readers' ability to use common sense and not put their faith in everything they read on the Internet!

LITTLE JACK HORNER

Little Jack Horner
Sat in the corner,
Eating a Christmas pie;
He put in his thumb,
And pulled out a plum,
And said, 'What a good boy am I!'

The inspiration behind 'Little Jack Horner' was Thomas Horner, steward to the Abbot of Glastonbury during the Dissolution of the Monasteries (1536–1540). 'Jack' was a colloquialism at the time for a knave, which we now use when referring to the knave in a pack of playing cards.

> A modern short story which redeems the character of Little Jack Horner somewhat is Neil Gaiman's 'The Case of the Four and Twenty Blackbirds'. Jack appears in the story, which also features a whole host of nursery rhyme characters, as a tough detective who investigates the murder of Humpty Dumpty.

In 1539, Glastonbury was the largest and richest abbey in England, and one of the last remaining Catholic strongholds. As the steward, Thomas Horner would have been responsible for collecting taxes, keeping accounts and managing the household.

In an attempt to save his abbey from destruction, the Abbott sent King Henry VIII a Christmas gift: the deeds to twelve manorial estates baked into a pie. As we see in 'Sing a Song of Sixpence', people would put all manner of unusual things into pies. There was a practical reason for this, as hiding valuables on a long and dangerous journey would have kept them safe from any potential bandits.

Horner was sent to deliver the pie to the king and, on the way, pulled out the proverbial 'plum' for himself – the deeds to the Manor of Mells in Somerset.

In the end, the Abbott's plan to appease the king ended in failure. He was tried for treason because of his loyalty to Rome. And who should have been on the jury that found him guilty? None other than Horner. The Abbot was sentenced to be hung, drawn and quartered, and Glastonbury Abbey was destroyed.

GEORGIE PORGIE

Georgie Porgie, pudding and pie,
Kissed the girls and made them cry;
When the boys came out to play,
Georgie Porgie ran away.

Georgie Porgie was the nickname of a Jacobean courtier, George Villiers, the First Duke of Buckingham (1592–1628). As well as being a notorious womaniser, he was also rumoured to be a lover of King James I. Certainly, the two men were close friends and the king held George in very high esteem, once remarking, 'Christ had John, and I have my George.'

George was described as being remarkably handsome, but he brought the Stuart house into disrepute with his bed-hopping antics. His best-known affair was with Anne of Austria, who was Queen Consort of France and married to Louis XIII. Their romance is documented in Alexander Dumas' novel *The Three Musketeers*.

A rapper from Houston in Texas, Devin the Dude, recorded a song 'Georgy' on his 1998 album *The Dude*. The line 'Georgie, Georgie, Kissed the girls and made them cry', is repeated as the chorus.

George was also unpopular in the Royal court and amongst the British people because he assisted in arranging the marriage of the king's son, Charles (later Charles I) to Princess Henrietta Maria – a French Catholic. Villiers' private life and his influence over the king enraged Parliament, and they eventually succeeded in banning James from intervening on George's behalf.

The behaviour of Georgie in the rhyme has outraged some modern critics, including a web writer called Burning Victory who, in the article 'Nursery Rhymes and Crime', views him as a coward who deserves to be slapped with a sexual harassment suit!

THREE BLIND MICE

Three blind mice, three blind mice.
See how they run, see how they run!
They all ran after the farmer's wife,
Who cut off their tails with a carving knife,
Did ever you see such a thing in your life,
As three blind mice?

This song seems gruesome enough in itself, but it actually refers to a rather bloody historical event: the execution of three Protestant bishops and noblemen at the request of Queen Mary I.

Despite a rather paltry record for executions compared to her father, Henry VIII, who had tens of thousands people put to death, the queen earned herself the unofficial title of 'Bloody Mary' due to her harsh persecution of the Protestant hierarchy. In an attempt to restore Roman Catholicism to the country, Mary condemned more than 300 Protestants to be burned at the stake; the same method of execution used in the Spanish Inquisition as a way of punishing heretics. Mary's husband, Philip II, was Spanish, and there was a real fear at the time that she would introduce her own English Inquisition.

It has been suggested that 'the farmer's wife' was a disrespectful reference to the queen, whose substantial estates throughout the country included many acres of farmland.

The three martyrs in the song were the Archbishop of Canterbury, Thomas Cranmer, Nicholas Ridley and Hugh Latimer. Accused of plotting against the queen and convicted of treason and heresy, in 1555 they were burned at the stake outside Balliol College, Oxford.

In sports games, including basketball and hockey, there are three referees, or umpires, who watch over the game, looking out for foul play. Sometimes 'Three Blind Mice' is used as a derogatory expression or chanted by the crowd if they think poor refereeing is taking place. Officially, however, this is frowned apon as unsportsmanlike.

OLD MOTHER HUBBARD

Old Mother Hubbard
Went to the cupboard,
To fetch her poor doggie a bone;
But when she got there
The cupboard was bare
And so the poor doggie had none.

The name Mother Hubbard is known to have been in existence since 1591, and there is speculation that the rhyme may have originally referred to Cardinal Thomas Wolsey and his failure to obtain a divorce from Queen Catherine of Aragon for Henry VIII – with Henry being the 'doggie', the divorce being the unobtainable 'bone', and the 'cupboard' representing the Catholic Church.

The first published example of this rhyme appeared in the 1805 edition of *The Comic Adventures of Old Mother Hubbard and Her Dog*, by Sarah Catherine Martin.

The author often visited the stately home of Kitley Manor in Devon, owned by her MP brother-in-law – the suitably named Sir Henry Bastard. Apparently inspired by a housekeeper at Kitley, Sarah told the rhyme to amuse her nieces and nephews.

The village of Yealmpton in Devon houses Old Mother Hubbard's stone cottage, now a popular tourist attraction.

MARY, MARY, QUITE CONTRARY

Mary, Mary, quite contrary,
How does your garden grow?
With silver bells and cockle shells,
And pretty maids all in a row.

This is another seemingly innocent nursery rhyme with a gruesome history which takes its inspiration from Queen Mary I. 'Silver bells and cockle shells' were slang terms for instruments of torture. The 'silver bells' were thumb screws used to crush the bones of the thumb – usually to extract a 'confession' from the victim – while cockleshells are believed to have been torture implements which were attached to the genitals (ouch!). The 'maids' or maidens might refer either to an early guillotine-like device used to behead people, or the 'iron maiden' – a notorious spiked contraption used in the medieval period.

Queen Mary, a Catholic, was desperate for England to remain a Catholic country after her death, and needed to produce an heir in order to stop her half-sister Elizabeth, a Protestant, becoming queen.

At the age of 37, Mary married Philip II of Spain, eleven years her junior. It was no secret that the marriage was more for the sake of political alliance between the two countries than for love. Mary held a thanksgiving service in 1554 to celebrate her first pregnancy, but the swelling in her belly turned out to be a cyst and she later suffered a second failed pregnancy.

Gossip about Mary's marriage and phantom pregnancies spread throughout the court. 'How does your garden grow?' could be a cruel reference to the queen's barren womb or marriage.

OLD KING COLE

Old King Cole
Was a merry old soul,
And a merry old soul was he;
He called for his pipe,
And he called for his bowl,
And he called for his fiddlers three.

Every fiddler, he had a fiddle,
And a very fine fiddle had he;
Oh, there's none so rare
As can compare
With King Cole and his fiddlers three.

The late American jazz singer-songwriter Nat King Cole (his real surname was Coles) admitted that he based his stage name on the 'merry old soul' of King Cole. Rock-pop band Genesis used 'Old King Cole' in the song 'The Musical Box', which featured on their album *Nursery Cryme*, released in 1971.

Old King Cole lends his name to Canadian tea brand 'King Cole', which has been produced by G. E. Barbour Inc. for a century or so.

This could be one of the oldest rhymes, however, as it recalls an ancient king of Celtic Britain. Cole is the Anglicised version of the Celtic word *Coel*, a Cumbric name, pronounced 'coil'. An Old King Cole is mentioned in Geoffrey of Monmouth's *Historia Regum Britanniae* as a king of the Britons. However, Geoffrey was writing in the twelfth century and his histories are nothing if not unreliable; many of the kings he wrote about (including King Arthur) are the stuff of legends, their actual existence unproven. So there is some dispute over Old King Cole's true identity. Was it…

… Coel Marius, a semi-mythic figure, about whom very little is known? If he existed, it was probably in the second century.

… Coel Godhebog, a Roman decurion who hailed from Colchester? He is reputed to have lived in the third century and his grandson was Emperor Constantine the Great.

… Cole Hen (Cole the Old)? He is the most likely real person and, due to his nickname, the most probable source of inspiration for the rhyme. Cole Hen reigned in the fifth century and lived to be 70 (which was ancient for the time).

The pipe that the king demands could be a musical instrument, a measure of wine, or a smoking pipe. If the latter, the song must originate from no earlier than the mid-1500s, when tobacco was introduced to Britain from the Americas. The nursery rhyme first appeared in print in 1709.

JACK AND JILL

Jack and Jill went up the hill
To fetch a pail of water;
Jack fell down and broke his crown,
And Jill came tumbling after.

Up Jack got, and home did trot,
As fast as he could caper,
He went to bed, and bound his head
With vinegar and brown paper.

One theory states that these lyrics refer to a pair of lovers, and serve as a warning to young people about the dangers of pre-marital sex.

The word 'tumble' was sixteenth-century slang and, according to Eric Partridge and Stanley Wells in *Bawdy Shakespeare*, meant to 'copulate' or 'play amorously'. This euphemism is frequently used by Shakespeare, as in this example from *Hamlet*: 'Quoth she, before you tumbled me, You promised me to wed.'

Jack's 'crown' is probably his cranium rather than any kind of elaborate headwear, as he nurses his injury at the end. Vinegar, due to its astringent properties, has been used for centuries as a cleaning product and to treat various ailments, although it is unlikely to have proven very effective for a fractured skull!

In Norse mythology, there is a story which bears some similarities to Jack and Jill: a brother and sister, Hjuki and Bil, are taken up from Earth to the Moon when fetching water from a well.

Some have said the rhyme refers to the executions of Louis XVI and his queen, Marie Antoinette, during the French Revolution and the Reign of Terror in 1793. However, the first publication date of the rhyme was in the John

Newbury book *Mother Goose's Melody* in the 1760s, which predates the events in France.

Jack and Jill is also a form of competitive dancing in America, in which couples are randomly matched, often with strangers, and have to dance to a piece of music unknown to them. It has proven popular at swing and ballroom dance competitions, and is designed to test dancers' social dancing skills. In the UK, this form of dancing is more commonly known as Dance With a Stranger (DWAS).

LITTLE BOY BLUE

Little Boy Blue,
Come blow your horn,
The sheep's in the meadow,
The cow's in the corn;
But where is the boy
Who looks after the sheep?
He's under a haycock,
Fast asleep.
Will you wake him?
No, not I,
For if I do,
He's sure to cry.

The rhyme describes a profession in the Middle Ages: that of the hayward, also known as a hedge-warden. These men were appointed by the lord of the manor to lead sowing and harvesting in the village, and to impound any stray cattle. The hayward's symbol of office was a horn, which he would have sounded to warn that cattle were invading the fields and eating the crops.

Another, perhaps more fanciful, explanation is that 'Little Boy Blue' was used in the Tudor period as a covert reference to Cardinal Thomas Wolsey (who certainly gets about a bit in the world of nursery rhymes!).

Cardinal Thomas Wolsey was sometimes known as the 'Boy Bachelor', after precociously winning an Oxford degree at the age of 15.

Wolsey was a generally unpopular figure at the time, who was well known for his immodest displays of wealth. Wool was incredibly important to England's economy, and the export trade in wool helped, in part, to make Henry VIII and Wolsey very rich. Wolsey's coat of arms consisted of four blue-faced leopards, which may account for the name 'little boy blue'.

Henry eventually tired of Wolsey and, in 1529, the king seized all his land and assets, following the failure of the

Cardinal to secure a divorce for Henry from his first wife, Catherine of Aragon. 'Where is the boy who looks after the sheep?' is perhaps a criticism of Wolsey putting his own interests before those of the people, his religious 'flock'.

ORANGES AND LEMONS

Oranges and lemons,
Say the bells of St Clement's.

You owe me five farthings,
Say the bells of St Martin's.

When will you pay me?
Say the bells of Old Bailey.

When I grow rich,
Say the bells of Shoreditch.

Pray when will that be?
Say the bells of Stepney.

I do not know,
Says the great bell at Bow.

Here comes a candle to light you to bed,
Here comes a chopper to chop off your head.

This nursery rhyme lists some of the most famous churches in the City of London. 'Oranges and Lemons' was also a square dance dating back to the mid-seventeenth century. The nursery rhyme appears in George Orwell's *Nineteen Eighty-Four* as a half-remembered ditty sung by the 'proles', which reminds the novel's hero, Winston Smith, of freer, more innocent times. Some of the churches mentioned are…

St Clement's: a small church in Eastcheap, the third to have stood on this site, now positioned between office blocks. The second building was destroyed in the Great Fire of London of 1666. When the River Thames was wider, citrus fruit cargoes from the Mediterranean landed at the wharf across the street. Some say that the church bells would ring when the fruit arrived. Another church, St Clement Danes, also lays claim to the origins of this reference, even having a yearly 'Oranges and Lemons' service. It has a connection with a fruit market, mentioned in *Pickwick Papers* by Charles Dickens.

St Martin's: St Martin Orgar in Martin Lane, an area that was notorious for money-lending. It was destroyed during the Great Fire and subsequently rebuilt. Then, in 1820, the church (except for the tower) was pulled down. The old bell was re-hung as a clock bell in St Clement's.

Old Bailey: St Sepulchre-without-Newgate is the largest church in London. Built around 1450, the tower holds the twelve bells of Old Bailey. The tenor bell was rung to signify that an execution was taking place in Newgate Prison, home to many criminals and debtors. The prison is now the site of the Old Bailey, the Central Criminal Court. St Sepulchre Church still houses the execution bell in a glass case.

Shoreditch: St Leonard's Church, now part of Hackney, was founded in the twelfth century in a poverty-stricken area – though Shoreditch has now grown rich, thanks to its proximity to the City of London financial district.

Bow: St Mary-le-Bow. During the fourteenth century, a curfew was imposed on the residents of Cheapside from 9 p.m. every night, which was announced by the pealing of Bow Bells. Famously, for someone to be able to call themselves a true Cockney, they must have been born within earshot of the Bow bells.

The final line could refer to the executions at the Tower of London, but there is a more bawdy theory. 'Here comes a candle to light you to bed' could be followed by a bride losing her 'maidenhead' or virginity, the 'chopper' being a crude description of the male appendage.

Some additional verses in longer versions of the rhyme:

Bull's eyes and targets,
Say the bells of St Margaret's

Brickbats and tiles,
Say the bells of St Giles

Two sticks and an apple,
Say the bells at Whitechapel

Old Father Baldpate,
Say the slow bells at Aldgate

Maids in white aprons,
Say the bells at St Catherine's

Pokers and tongs,
Say the bells at St John's

Kettles and pans,
Say the bells of St Anne's…

DOCTOR FOSTER

Doctor Foster went to Gloucester
In a shower of rain;
He stepped in a puddle,
Right up to his middle,
And never went there again.

> The nursery rhyme may have acted as a precautionary tale for children to be careful of puddles, in the days before modern roads, as they might have been much deeper and more dangerous than they appeared on first sight.

Gloucester is situated on the banks of the River Severn and, unfortunately, is prone to flooding. When visiting in the thirteenth century, King Edward I fell off his horse into a deep, muddy puddle during a rainstorm. The locals used planks of wood to rescue king and horse from the mire, but Edward was apparently so enraged he refused to ever visit Gloucester again.

It must have been a fairly deep puddle, as King Edward was a man of intimidating stature, nicknamed Longshanks due to his height. In 1774, the Society of Antiquaries opened his coffin and revealed the body of the king, which had been preserved over centuries. They measured him at six feet two inches – pretty impressive when the average male height during the thirteenth century was five foot seven. Edward, played by Patrick McGoohan, is portrayed as a cruel tyrant in the 1995 film *Braveheart*.

Why King Edward would be called Doctor Foster is unclear, and whether or not the king did visit Gloucester is unknown. The only true historical connection we know of was the Statute of Gloucester which Edward passed in 1278, when he tried to regulate the power of the feudal lords.

POP! GOES THE WEASEL

Half a pound of tuppenny rice,
Half a pound of treacle.
That's the way the money goes,
Pop! goes the weasel.

Some of us remember additional verses:

> All around the mulberry bush,
> The monkey chased the weasel.
> The monkey stopped to scratch his nose,
> Pop! goes the weasel.

> Half a pound of tuppenny rice,
> Half a pound of treacle.
> Mix it up and make it nice,
> Pop! goes the weasel.

> Up and down the City road,
> In and out the Eagle.
> That's the way the money goes,
> Pop! goes the weasel.

> Every time when I come home,
> The monkey's on the table.
> Take a stick and knock it off,
> Pop! goes the weasel.

Originating from the eighteenth-century East End of London, 'Pop! Goes the Weasel' uses Cockney rhyming slang as a way of satirising the effects of poverty. 'Pop' meant to pawn something, while weasel could be a coat (as in 'weasel and stoat') or a corruption of 'whistle' which means suit (from 'whistle and flute'). Either way, the phrase describes the pawning of your best clothes in order to buy foodstuffs such as rice and treacle.

Even poor people would have had something smart to wear when attending church – their 'Sunday best'. The idea of spending too much money and having to sell your clothes, only to buy them back again the next week, might have been an endless, frustrating cycle for some families.

What about the monkey? 'Monkey' is believed to be a nineteenth-century term for a pub drinking vessel, and a 'stick' is a shot of alcohol. So 'take a stick and knock it off' was a description of drinking in the pub – a good way of losing money!

The Eagle was a pub on the corner of City Road in Hackney, North London. In 1825 it was rebuilt as a music hall, which Charles Dickens was known to frequent.

US newspapers referred to 'Pop! Goes the Weasel' as 'the latest English dance' in the 1850s, while a newspaper advertisement in 1854 referred to it as a new country dance introduced by Queen Victoria. 'Pop! Goes the

Weasel' was shouted enthusiastically at certain points during the dance.

In the US, the phrase stuck. A newspaper advertisement from *The Hudson North Star* in 1856 said: 'All selling cheap. To close out within sixty days or pop goes the weasel.'

SIMPLE SIMON

Simple Simon met a pieman,
Going to the fair;
Says Simple Simon to the pieman,
Let me taste your ware.

Says the pieman to Simple Simon,
Show me first your penny;
Says Simple Simon to the pieman,
Indeed I have not any.

Simple Simon went a-fishing,
For to catch a whale;
All the water he had got
Was in his mother's pail.

Simple Simon went to look
If plums grew on a thistle;
He pricked his fingers very much,
Which made poor Simon whistle.

He went for water in a sieve
But soon it all fell through;
And now poor Simple Simon
Bids you all 'Adieu'.

The tradition of fairs dates back to medieval England. Vendors set out stalls along the route selling trays of food or wares – a bit like modern-day burger vans.

The tale of Simple Simon, called 'Simple Simon's Misfortune' appeared in an Elizabethan chapbook – a small pamphlet containing folk tales and songs sold by pedlars called chapmen.

The character of Simple Simon became the butt of the joke in some pantomimes, especially *Mother Goose*. Simon may have been the common name for a simpleton for centuries, perhaps even dating back to the biblical stories of the fisherman St Peter (who changed his name from Simon), as the Simon in the rhyme makes a laughable attempt to fish. It isn't certain if simple meant ordinary or humble, as in 'simple folk', or if poor Simon was of less-than-average intelligence. The third and fourth verses seem to indicate that it's the latter and not the most politically correct of nursery rhymes!

Nevertheless, Simon seems to display a certain level of sophistication when he uses the French word 'adieu' for goodbye. There was a strong French influence in medieval England following the Norman Conquest of 1066, and French was considered a prestige language amongst the upper classes.

LITTLE TOMMY TUCKER

Little Tommy Tucker,
Sings for his supper:
What shall we give him?
White bread and butter.
How shall he cut it
Without a knife?
How will he be married
Without a wife?

'Little Tommy Tucker' was included in *Tom Thumb's (Pretty) Song Book*, published in London in 1744.

> Little Tommy Tucker is also the name of a miniature yellow rose bred in America by Robert Tucker.

'Tommy Tucker' was a colloquial term for the orphans who lived on the streets of the cities during the eighteenth and nineteenth centuries. Extreme poverty meant that these children were forced to beg, and would often have to literally sing for their suppers. By entertaining and amusing the richer residents with their vocal talents, the orphans would try to earn enough money to buy enough food to stay alive.

The last two lines refer to the orphans' meagre possessions, which would have made it difficult to marry. Inheritance and family 'name' were hugely important in the Georgian and Victorian eras and, with no connections or wealth, the orphans had little chance of ever being wed.

LONDON BRIDGE

London Bridge is falling down,
Falling down, falling down,
London Bridge is falling down,
My fair lady.

Build it up with wood and clay,
Wood and clay, wood and clay,
Build it up with wood and clay,
My fair lady.

Wood and clay will wash away,
Wash away, wash away,
Wood and clay will wash away,
My fair lady.

Build it up with bricks and mortar,
Bricks and mortar, bricks and mortar,
Build it up with bricks and mortar,
My fair lady.

Bricks and mortar will not stay,
Will not stay, will not stay,
Bricks and mortar will not stay,
My fair lady.

Build it up with iron and steel,
Iron and steel, iron and steel,
Build it up with iron and steel,
My fair lady.

Iron and steel will bend and bow,
Bend and bow, bend and bow,
Iron and steel will bend and bow,
My fair lady.

Build it up with silver and gold,
Silver and gold, silver and gold,
Build it up with silver and gold,
My fair lady.

Silver and gold will be stolen away,
Stolen away, stolen away,
Silver and gold will be stolen away,
My fair lady.

Set a man to watch all night,
Watch all night, watch all night,
Set a man to watch all night,
My fair lady.

Suppose the man should fall asleep,
Fall asleep, fall asleep,
Suppose the man should fall asleep?
My fair lady.

Give him a pipe to smoke all night,
Smoke all night, smoke all night,
Give him a pipe to smoke all night,
My fair lady.

A bridge has stood on or near the present site of London Bridge since the Roman occupation almost 2,000 years ago, and 'My Fair Lady' describes the problems encountered over the centuries when attempting to bridge the River Thames. The early structures had to be rebuilt many times, and were beset by disasters, including fire and destruction by a Viking invasion. The first stone version took 33 years to build in the twelfth century. By the 1300s, the bridge housed more than 100 large shops; 'silver and gold' could allude to the commerce that flourished there.

This bridge survived the Great Fire of London in 1666, but in 1831 it was pulled down and a new London Bridge was constructed on a different site. In 1968, this was sold to American entrepreneur Robert P. McCulloch of McCulloch Oil. The bridge was dismantled stone by stone and transferred to Lake Havasu in Arizona in the United States. The London Bridge which straddles the Thames today was built in the 1960s.

> T. S. Eliot used the opening two lines of the nursery rhyme in his iconic poem 'The Waste Land'.

In an alternative version of the rhyme, there is a verse with the line 'Take a key and lock her up'. This might refer to an ancient and grisly superstition of burying a dead virgin under the foundations of bridges in order to strengthen them through magic. Others have posited that the 'fair lady' was Eleanor of Aquitaine, who married King Henry

II and was one of the most powerful women in Europe during the Middle Ages.

The 1993 film *Falling Down*, starring Michael Douglas, was also inspired by the song. Douglas' character buys his daughter a snow-shaker which plays the tune, and the wife of the detective repeatedly states that she wants to retire to Lake Havasu City, where the old London Bridge now stands.

JACK SPRAT

Jack Sprat could eat no fat,
His wife could eat no lean,
And so between them both, you see,
They licked the platter clean.

Here are some additional verses:

> Jack ate all the lean,
> Joan ate all the fat,
> The bone they picked it clean,
> Then gave it to the cat
>
> Jack Sprat was wheeling,
> His wife by the ditch,
> The barrow turned over,
> And in she did pitch.
>
> Says Jack, 'She'll be drowned!',
> But Joan did reply,
> 'I don't think I shall,
> For the ditch is quite dry.'

Many say Jack Sprat refers to King Charles I and his queen, Henrietta Maria of France. Parliament refused to finance Charles' war against Spain, so his wife imposed an illegal war tax – thus boosting their profits – after an angry Charles dissolved Parliament.

Another interpretation is that it recalls the story of Richard the Lionheart and his brother, King John. In 1189, John (Jack Sprat) married the daughter of the Earl of Gloucester,

Isabel (who was also known by several alternative names, including Hawise, Eleanor and Joan). Isabel was described as being 'ambitious and greedy'.

On returning from the Crusades, King Richard was kidnapped and John was forced to pay the ransom of 150,000 marks, which left the country impoverished for years afterwards – which might account for the idea of licking 'the platter clean'. When John was crowned king, his marriage to Isabel (Joan) was annulled on the grounds of consanguinity, meaning that they shared the same bloodline, and she was never recognised as queen.

Jack Sprat might have been a nickname for people of short stature in the sixteenth and seventeenth centuries. It can also be a derogatory term for couples in which the man is skinny and the woman overweight.

MARY HAD A LITTLE LAMB

Mary had a little lamb,
Its fleece was white as snow;
And everywhere that Mary went
The lamb was sure to go.

He followed her to school one day,
That was against the rule;
It made the children laugh and play
To see a lamb at school.

And so the teacher turned it out,
But still it lingered near,
And waited patiently about
Till Mary did appear.

Why does the lamb love Mary so?
The eager children cry;
Why, Mary loves the lamb, you know,
The teacher did reply.

First published as a poem in 1830 by Sara Josepha Hale, this poem can be taken fairly literally. Mary Sawyer attended Redstone School in Sterling, Massachussets and, after some encouragement from her brother, decided to take her lamb to school.

Some believe that the original first four lines were composed by young John Roulstone, a nephew of a visiting priest who was at the school the day Mary brought in her lamb, with Hale adding the extra lines at the end.

Even the music industry has found a place for Mary and her lamb: the rock band Evanescence played around with the lyrics in their song 'Lose Control', as did Smashing Pumpkins in 'X.Y.U.'

The inventor Thomas Edison used the first stanza of this rhyme when testing his newly invented phonograph in 1877. He recorded it onto tinfoil wrapped round a grooved cylinder. The scratchy recording is credited as the second audio recording to have been made and played back.

More recently, the rhyme has been used in television science fiction programmes such as *Babylon 5* and *Alpha Centauri*. By concentrating on the rhyme as a mantra, characters have the power to block out intrusive telepathy from their enemies.

WEE WILLIE WINKIE

Wee Willie Winkie runs through the town,
Up stairs and down stairs in his night-gown,
Rapping at the window, crying at the lock,
Are the children all in bed, for now it's eight
o'clock?

'Wee Willie Winkie' was written in 1841 by William Miller, originally in Scots dialect. The full poem is five verses long, but most people only remember the first.

In a time when there was a significant political struggle over civil liberties, and the police force was still relatively new, curfews were introduced 'for the good of the people'. This conflicted with the liberal values of many, who believed that when they went to bed was nobody's business but their own. Wee Willie Winkie in his night-gown provided an ironic image of the police force, rushing around trying to enforce a strict curfew.

Wee Willie Winkie is also believed by many to have been the inspiration for the famous Public Service Announcement in America, 'It's 10 p.m., do you know where your children are?' These announcements ran from the 1960s through to 2003, and were parodied in the cult TV series *The Simpsons*.

LADYBIRD, LADYBIRD, FLY AWAY HOME

Ladybird, ladybird,
Fly away home,
Your house is on fire
And your children all gone;

All except one
And that's little Ann
And she has crept under
The warming pan.

Having a ladybird land on you was, and still is, considered to be very lucky but, if it did not fly off, it was customary to gently blow it away. 'Ladybird, Ladybird' is recited by children when a ladybird lands on them, to encourage it to fly away.

Ladybirds come in all different shapes, sizes and colours. A red ladybird with black spots is the most common type but you may, if you're lucky, see the rarer yellow one with black spots.

Ladybirds appear in Britain's countryside over the summer months and it became a tradition for farmers to call out 'Ladybird, ladybird' before clearing the fields after harvest. Farmers appreciate the ladybird's worth, as they feed on aphids, so helping to reduce the numbers on their crops. Perhaps for this reason children were discouraged from harming ladybirds, and the myth arose that it was bad luck to kill them.

The word ladybird also has connotations with the Catholic name for the mother of Jesus, 'Our Lady'. The Act of Uniformity of 1559 and 1662 demanded that Catholics attend Protestant services; Catholic priests were forbidden to say Mass and followers were not allowed to attend. If priests broke the law, typically this meant being burnt at the stake. The rhyme could have been used as a threat to any wayward Catholics.

Guy Fawkes was, almost certainly, the most famous Catholic recusant, and there is perhaps some link between the ladybird's house being on fire and the Houses of Parliament being set alight.

The American word for ladybird is 'ladybug'. In the US, 'firebug' is slang for an arsonist, so this would relate to the house being on fire.

ROCK-A-BYE, BABY

Rock-a-bye, baby, on the tree top,
When the wind blows the cradle will rock;
When the bough breaks the cradle will fall,
And down will come baby, cradle, and all.

One reading of this rhyme is that it describes the observations of an American pilgrim boy, who noticed how Native North American Wampanoag women, working in fields, would hang a birch-bark cradle from a tree branch and allow the wind to rock the baby to sleep. 'When the bough breaks the cradle will fall' cautions that choosing a strong branch was imperative.

The original version of the rhyme, published in 1765, began with the line 'Hush-a-bye, baby', but after Al Jolson released the hit 1918 song 'Rock-a-bye Your Baby with a Dixie Melody', the lyrics became corrupted to 'Rock-a-bye, baby'.

Another interpretation is that it derives from the lifestyle of a Kenyan family in eighteenth-century England. While working as charcoal burners in the Shining Cliff Woods in Ambergate, Derbyshire, the family made their house inside a huge, 2,000-year-old yew tree, known as 'Betty Kenny Tree'. The main bough of the tree was hollowed out and used as a cradle for the family's eight children. The yew tree is still in existence but was seriously damaged by fire in the 1930s, when it was targeted by arsonists.

'Rock-a-bye, Baby' is often sung to a baby whilst being rocked, to lull the child to sleep. When teaching the nursery rhyme to children, they are shown how to make a rocking motion with their arms, mimicking a mother and her baby. However, the change at the end of the song to something more sinister, 'And down will come baby, cradle, and all', is typical of other nursery rhymes which, using distorted fragments of old songs or ballads, conjure an almost forgotten dangerous past.

Other titles from Summersdale

THINGS WE USED TO BELIEVE

Sam Foster

ISBN: 978 84024 532 5   Hardback   £6.99

Cats were female and dogs were male.

If you put a tape recorder in an aquarium,
you could hear the fish speak.

You could sail to Japan on a rice paper boat
with rice paper sheets and rice paper plates.
And then eat it all when you arrived.

This selection of insights into the unique and often hilarious
child's eye view of the world is guaranteed to charm and
bewilder in equal measure.

Peculiar proverbs

weird words of wisdom from around the world.

Stephen Arnott

PECULIAR PROVERBS
Weird Words of Wisdom From Around the World

Stephen Arnott

ISBN: 978 84024 619 3   Hardback   £9.99

'With patience and saliva, the ant swallows the elephant.'
COLOMBIAN

'Never bolt your door with a boiled carrot.'
IRISH

'Badly cut hair is two men's shame.'
DANISH

This collection of genuine proverbs from cultures around the world ignores the common sayings we all know and concentrates on the unusual. Some are deft, witty and colourful, others plain weird. But they're all fascinating. With topics such as Wisdom and Discretion, Law and Order, Work (and Reasons Not To) and Love and Marriage, these quirky sayings provide much food for thought about human nature.

Peculiar Proverbs includes sayings you won't find in any other collection, sometimes so surreal they defy you to decipher them, providing hours of entertainment. Remember: *The man who tickles himself can laugh when he chooses.*

www.summersdale.com